Jimmy Stewart

A LIFE IN PICTURES

Jimmy Stewart

A LIFE IN PICTURES

ELLEN VON KARAJAN

MetroBooks

MetroBooks

An Imprint of Friedman/Fairfax Publishers

Library of Congress Cataloging-in-Publication Data available upon request.
ISBN 1-56799-647-7

Editor: Emily Zelner
Art Director: Jeff Batzli
Layout Designer: Christina Grupico
Photography Editor: Valerie E. Kennedy
Production Manager: Ingrid Neimanis-McNamara

Color separations by Ocean Graphic International Company Ltd.
Printed in China by Leefung-Asco Printers Ltd.

1 3 5 7 9 10 8 6 4 2

For bulk purchases and special sales, please contact:
Friedman/Fairfax Publishers
Attention: Sales Department
15 West 26th Street
New York, NY 10010
212/685-6610   FAX 212/685-1307

Visit our website:
http://www.metrobooks.com

Dedication

This book is dedicated to my parents, Howard and Margaret, on the occasion of their 50th wedding anniversary.

Acknowledgments

The author wishes to acknowledge the following individuals for sharing information, anecdotes and/or visual materials or for providing inspiration and encouragement:

Karena Lingenfelter Adams, Janet Amick, Mary Ann Ballard, Dr. Madan and Mrs. Seema Batra, Bonnie Polito Battick, Sally and the late Keith Bloom, Gemma Boyer, Christine Brownlee, Dr. Carol Butzow, Margaret Cavill, Ian Flynn, Ted and Mark von Gatbless, Jim Gladkosky, Peggy and Carson Greene, Jr., Sister Carol Grimes, Tom Harley, Ken Hayden, Frank Hood, Connie Howard, Liz and Kay Hutton, Kim Hoff, Allison McCoy Jones, Dr. Krish Krishnan, Kenan Kavank, Kim and Roxanne of Rouki's, Terry and Johanna Leach, Liz Lepper, Janie McKirgan, J. Collum McPhermus, S. J., Linda Moore-Mack, Frank Moore, the late Bill Moorhead, Dr. Steve Osborne, Barbara Rago, Ed Ruffner, Bruce and Elizabeth Salome, Stephanie, Katrina Sexton, Barbara Shaffer, Dr. Kevin Stemmler, George Stewart, Joe Stuber, Phil Zorich.

The following organizations also provided assistance and information:
Indiana University of Pennsylvania, Mercersberg Academy, Princeton University, The Genealogical and Historical Society of Indiana County, The Indiana Gazette, WDAD Radio.

These individuals shared their memories, reflections, experience, and insights and gave me new ways of "seeing" Jimmy Stewart, either in the mind's or heart's eye, or visually:

June Allyson, Janice Ambrose, Jonathan Baird, Paul Ben-Zvi, Elinor Blair, Nick Clooney, Scott Decker, Gary Fishgall, Marion Grelle, Kelly Harcourt, Rex Hardy, Dr. Ron Juliette, Janet Leigh, Kelly Moore, Frank Shaffer, Judy Merrill, Michael Mikisel, Gerard Molyneaux, Chuck Olson, Mary Martha Pulick, Cheri Pederson, Stacey Perrot, and through her, the late Rosamond Quinn, Clarence Stephenson, John D. Varner

Thanks to Anne Hutton who helped assemble and verify the chronologies and the reference materials.

Special thanks, too, to Tony and Helen Lenzi and to Ed and CeCe Mackey for their encouragement and support and for showing a woman from Baltimore, through their own genuine kindness, spirit and hard work, that special "something" that the community of Indiana, Pennsylvania had contributed to the development of Jimmy Stewart's greatness.

CONTENTS

Introduction

Opposite: Jimmy Stewart was a gentleman, born and bred. As he matured, and particularly after his return from World War II, he acquired an enormous dignity of bearing and depth of expression, captured in this photo portrait. Though he was a master comic and quipster who loved to play to the camera, he had a very serious side to his personality and was shy, reserved and self contained throughout his long life. The tweed jacket was a staple in his wardrobe—it added bulk to his frame, suited his Ivy League upbringing, and wore like iron (an important feature for a man who hated shopping and couldn't see spending a lot of money on clothes).

Above: What *did* the dummy say to Jimmy? Jimmy spent more than his fair share of time with dummies, particularly after he was promoted to second lieutenant in the Army Air Corps. Instead of sending him overseas, the military kept him stateside to recruit and entertain troops. The 1940s were the heyday of Edgar Bergen's Charlie McCarthy, and Jimmy played the straight man to their jokes almost daily for a three month period in 1941, in addition to a number of radio appearances they made together at other points in their careers.

Right: The Stewart Family: Jimmy and Gloria with her sons, Michael and Ron, and the twins, Judy and Kelly. Jimmy Stewart's legacy as a parent is perhaps his least well known, but anyone who has met his children would agree they weathered his celebrity well and grew up to become intelligent, expressive, and thoughtful people.

Jimmy Stewart the child was truly father to the man. He loved animals, the great outdoors, aviation, invention and technology, performing and stunts, music, and magic. What struck people about him early on, besides his gangly build, was his quixotic imagination and the quirky intelligence that gave it form, whether he was building crystal radio sets, play-acting, or launching a passenger off the Whizzbang (a thrill ride he invented that relied on gravity, a slanted roof, and a rope with an attached seat). He seemed as unassuming, plain-spoken, and down-home as the boy next door. Reared in a small town in Pennsylvania, he was gentle and soft-spoken, but he was also a highly intelligent prep school and Ivy League graduate. All of his boyhood passions would find fuller expression in his film career, but it was the practice of magic that breathed life into his films for more than sixty years of cinema.

Magic has two faces: a performance aspect that creates illusions by sleight of hand and another, more mysterious, Merlin-like aspect that includes the ability to conjure, invoke, and cast binding spells. Jimmy Stewart was a master of both. He was employed as an actor and entertainer, but he was practicing his own form of magic through more than six decades and eighty films.

Just as a good magician knows precisely how to invoke the spirits to do his bidding, Jimmy Stewart knew how to invoke the Muses to bind his audience in his spell. The illusions and emotions he created on film were so real that as viewers of Jimmy Stewart's films we hold some of them as our very own memories.

What he loved about Cecil B. DeMille, the famous producer and director with a no-nonsense reputation as a stern taskmaster, was that "he was always conscious of the set *as a place of magic*. He played it to the hilt, and to the benefit of everyone." Jimmy was so eager to work with this kindred spirit on *The Greatest Show on Earth* (1952) that he took a 75 percent cut in his usual salary, settled for last billing—"And James Stewart as Buttons the Clown"—at the height of his career, and never once was seen in the film without his clown makeup.

Another part of the magic was Jimmy's agility at making it look so easy and natural—this business of acting, this art of performing onscreen. This is not to say that he ever claimed the title of artist for himself; he didn't. Jimmy certainly didn't seem to approach acting as an art. He did not study it in any formal setting (he had majored in architecture at Princeton), nor did he practice what is known as the Method, an acting system originated by Konstantin

Stanislavsky that emphasizes eliciting the imagination of the actor, whereby the actor practically becomes the character he is going to play.

Jimmy once said, "The most important thing about acting is to approach it as a craft, not as an art and not as some mysterious type of religion. Acquiring the skill is what acting is all about. The thing is to be able to do a part and not have the acting show." He did not let the audience know that he had learned early in his career to perform as though his viewers were "partners and not customers"; that Spencer Tracy had taught him to "forget the camera"; and that Marlene Dietrich had told him how to avoid distraction and eyestrain in an over-the-shoulder shot—"Look into one eye or the other of your partner onscreen but never into both at the same time." These camera tricks and points of the actor's craft impressed him sufficiently that he talked about them in a number of interviews throughout the years, as if they were major elements in his success as an actor.

When it came to revealing the details of how he approached a role—what he put himself through to define the character and to perfect the nuances of his expression—he didn't have much to say. But he did plenty, and there wasn't much magic about what he did,

just a lot of hard work. He did his homework from the very beginning of his career, when the studio system couldn't quite figure out how to cast him. W.S. Van Dyke, a director at MGM, looked at Jimmy's screen tests and called him "unusually usual," sensing there was something special but uncertain about what to do with it.

Lean and tall, with a straightforward face and clear, earnest eyes, Jimmy didn't seem to fit the profile of a movie actor at all, so every role was an experiment, every part a chance to prove himself and find his type. So he put himself through the paces from the very beginning.

For example, he didn't relax much on the set between takes. If he did, he read only the lightest of fare (Flash Gordon comics were a favorite in his younger days) so that he wouldn't be distracted. By his own admission, he wasn't a quick study when it came to learning his lines, so he immersed himself in his character and concentrated solely on how he would portray it in the next scene. This most congenial and seemingly easygoing man was a highly disciplined perfectionist and very particular about his every word, expression, and move onscreen.

What he could not manage to convey while acting through his craft and various camera tricks he looked for in chemicals, prosthetics,

Above: Jimmy, as Elwood P. Dowd, martini aficionado and "pixilated" philosopher, with a costumer's rendition of Harvey, the great white rabbit. Jimmy's own sketches tell us that he saw Harvey as a far more imposing, independent, compelling, and complex figure. Years later, in 1990, Jimmy would describe his impressions of Harvey, the character *and* the film, in a video introduction featuring clips from the film and his voice-over. This became a best-selling MCA video release, kept Stewart in the limelight, and introduced him to a new generation who had known him previously only as George Bailey in *It's a Wonderful Life*.

and props. He had a doctor coat his throat with bichloride of mercury after director Frank Capra told him he didn't have quite the right depth to his hoarseness in the filibuster scene in *Mr. Smith Goes to Washington* (1939). He had his hair, eyebrows, and eyelashes dyed blonde to more closely resemble Charles Lindbergh in *The Spirit of St. Louis* (1957). As Mattie Appleyard in *Fool's Parade* (1971), he wore a glass eye (actually a huge contact lens), which he takes out and brandishes in one memorable scene when he wanted to add dramatic impact to his character.

He prepared in other ways, too. During the filming of *The Glenn Miller Story* (1954), Jimmy read Miller's diaries and letters, met extensively with his widow, listened to all of his recordings, and watched everything he could find about the famous bandleader on film. Then he tried to learn to play the trombone. Joe Yukl, a professional musician with a sensitive ear, was hired to teach him.

Jimmy already knew how to play the piano, the banjo, the ukulele, and the accordion, so he felt he would be able to learn the trombone without too much difficulty. He applied himself to his lessons and practiced diligently, but to no avail. He was so bad that Yukl threatened to quit. They finally settled on an arrangement wherein his teacher stayed on as his advisor on the film and Jimmy plugged the bell so that it was impossible for any of the sounds he made to come through.

But if Jimmy's efforts to play the trombone had distressed Yukl, the frustrated teacher was definitely impressed by what he saw on the set: "He blew out his lip on the mouthpiece, crossed his legs musician-style, fiddled around with the spit-valve, then picked up the chorus right on the beat. Suddenly, I felt like I was looking in a mirror. Jimmy had been studying my mannerisms while I taught him how to play the trombone, and when the cameras turned he put them to use. He's the most thorough guy I've ever known."

Directors who observed Jimmy in scenes that were shot more than once reported that when they thought he was just "playing himself"—reacting and gesturing spontaneously on camera—he would confound them with exact repetitions in every take. He had an almost uncanny command of his facial expressions and gestures. What amazed students of his performances was the very deliberate plan for when and where to use these gestures. There wasn't a blink of his eye or a turn of his chin he hadn't plotted out in advance.

If Paul Muni was the man of a thousand faces, Jimmy Stewart was surely the face with a thousand expressions. Perhaps that was

why Alfred Hitchcock wanted him for *Rear Window* (1954). Confined to a wheelchair throughout the entire film, Jimmy's face, gestures, and voice were *all* he had to work with. He had to act and react with total credibility. Jimmy did, right down to making us feel the itch under the cast on his leg.

Costars who closely studied his performances observed that he would never "go over the top," that is, overemote or ham it up. Actor Ben Gazzara, himself trained in the Method and two decades younger than Jimmy when they worked on *Anatomy of a Murder* (1959) together, said of Jimmy's performance simply that "he had all the moves." In a sorrowful moment, he would let the tears well up in his eyes, but he would stop short of weeping. Not that he underacted—he didn't. He was confident and experienced and comfortable enough in front of the camera to know that his audience would feel his emotions, whatever they were.

There was magic in his voice, too. He delivered his lines, comic and dramatic, in a halting, almost folksy voice and with a particular diction that were as uniquely his own as his facial expressions and bearing. We always believed what he said, as though a man with a voice like that had to be "for real." We believed him in zany roles in madcap comedies and in intense roles in serious dramas. In fact, his last film featured just his voice as Wiley E. Burp in the cartoon *An American Tail: Fievel Goes West* (1990).

Jimmy Stewart knew there was magic in his medium and in his performances and that he gave people something extraordinary and durable to hold on to long after they left the theater. That was what he loved about his work more than anything else. "Moments," he once said, "little pieces of time—that's what everyone is trying to create in the moving-picture business. Even now, people will walk up to me and say, about a film that's twenty years old, 'I don't remember the name of the movie, but I remember this scene, and you said...and it was really good....' and, well I remembered it too and I thought it was pretty good and that's been the wonderful thing about this career. I've given people little pieces of time they have remembered for twenty years."

Most of us knew him only as an image and a voice on celluloid, yet Jimmy Stewart *seemed* more real to us than most of our neighbors, more real than any of a hundred other brightly shining stars in the constellation of Hollywood. That was his ultimate mastery of illusion: a magic that promises to live on as long as his films are shown.

Chapter One

A Portrait of the Artist as a Young Man

Opposite: Jimmy and his mother. The oldest child of Alexander (Alec) Stewart and Elizabeth (Bessie) Jackson Stewart, Jimmy was born on May 20, 1908, in "the Garden of Eden," the name his parents had given their first home in Indiana, Pennsylvania. Jimmy's birth weight was a hefty eight pounds (3.5kg). Bessie was an accomplished musician who had given recitals of Beethoven and Mendelssohn when she was a student at Wilson College. The daughter of Colonel Samuel Jackson, a Union hero who also served as treasurer for the Commonwealth of Pennsylvania, she was the church organist. Music and singing were always focal points of the family's time together. Forever a devoted son, Jimmy was at her side in Indiana when she died at age seventy-eight.

Above: Jimmy and Dotie, one of his two sisters. Mary (Dotie) Wilson Stewart was born on January 12, 1912, and Virginia Kelly Stewart was born on October 29, 1914. The Stewart family earned a comfortable income from their hardware store, and the children were always dressed to a tee in the fashion of the times and were notably well behaved.

Above: Three generations of Stewarts stand in front of the family hardware store, J.M. Stewart and Company. Jimmy was named for his paternal grandfather, who had fought in the Civil War with the Signal Corps at the battles of Winchester, Fisher's Hill, and Cedar Creek. Jimmy's father, a Princeton graduate, had fought in the Spanish-American War and World War I and was a staunch Presbyterian. He was active in many community organizations, most notably the volunteer fire association. The hardware store was the scene of many of Jimmy's fondest childhood memories and Alec hoped for years that his son would one day return to run the family business because he never considered "play-acting" an honorable or suitable career for his son.

Left: Jimmy in the parlor. The family moved to 104 North Seventh Street, in the Vinegar Hill section of Indiana, in 1914. This was to be the family home until Jimmy's father died in 1968. The house was chosen because of its proximity to the local fire station and the hardware store, both located just blocks away. Here Jimmy, his sisters, and their neighbors began producing small plays, among them *To Hell with the Kaiser*, which Jimmy wrote, produced, and starred in when he was ten years old.

Right: Each of the Stewart children studied at least one musical instrument. Jimmy learned to play the piano, banjo, ukulele, and accordion, the latter "so it would not go to waste" when his father accepted the instrument as payment for a debt. At that time, Jimmy was a student at the Model School, now Wilson Hall, on the University of Pennsylvania's Indiana campus. He attended the Model School through the ninth grade. By the time he advanced to the Mercersburg Academy in Mercersburg, Pennsylvania, he played the accordion well enough to perform in the school's Marshall Orchestra.

Above: In his senior year at Princeton, Jimmy played the part of Alfonso the strolling troubadour in *Spanish Blades*. He also became involved in cheerleading and in the more serious dramas produced by Princeton's Theatre Intime, such as *Nerissa*. Despite his increasing involvement and pleasure in performing, he insisted that he would pursue graduate studies in architecture.

Below: Though taken years after his graduation, this photo evokes memories of Jimmy's college days. At Princeton, he was drawn to the Triangle Club, one of the oldest undergraduate theater groups in the country. (Many of the student members of the club at that time, including José Ferrar, Josh Logan, and Myron McCormick, were already intent on careers on stage and screen.) Jimmy also established a reputation as a vocalist and in 1929 he joined the Charter Club, which sponsored jazz weekends with some of the biggest names in the business. He sometimes sang with Ferrar's dance band, the Pied Pipers. Ferrar was to feature prominently in Jimmy's life again many years later. In 1950, both were nominated for Academy Awards for Best Actor—Ferrar for his portrayal of the title role in *Cyrano de Bergerac* and Jimmy for his signature role as Elwood P. Dowd in *Harvey*. Ferrar won.

Chapter Two

Jimmy on Stage and Screen

Opposite: Jimmy was equally effective as the down-home boy and the suave sophisticate, as shown in this photo, which may have been taken during his work in the early 1930s with the University Players, a summer stock group located in Falmouth, Massachusetts, whose talent consisted primarily of aspiring college students. Buddy Josh Logan had been relentless in his efforts to persuade Jimmy to join this group—not because of Jimmy's acting abilities, but so that he could play the accordion as an important addition to the supper club entertainment in the tearoom. He also designed sets, worked as a stagehand, had a few walk-on parts—and met Henry Fonda for the first time.

Above: Jimmy in *Yellow Jack* (1934) at the Martin Beck Theater in New York City. His role in *Yellow Jack* won him a screen test with MGM that finally resulted in a contract of $350 a week for seven years, renewable every six months. He had already screen-tested with Fox and Warner Brothers; Warner cast him in *Art Trouble* (1934), a two-reel comedy with Shemp Howard of the Three Stooges. Jimmy's performance, all arms and legs, did not win him a contract, but it marked his debut on film.

Right: In his junior year, Jimmy and producer-director Josh Logan appeared together in *The Tiger Smiles*. Logan said he had written the juvenile lead for Jimmy because of his "droll Pennsylvania drawl." Stewart is shown here with Logan (center) and Marshall Dana in the Triangle Club's 1930 production.

Left: When Jimmy first came to Hollywood, MGM could not figure out how to cast him: was he a comic actor or a romantic lead? The studio was already rich with talent and great leading men, such as Clark Gable, Robert Taylor, Spencer Tracy, and Lionel Barrymore, so it decided to begin with a Chick Sales comic short, *Important News* (1935).

Above: Fan magazines began building Jimmy's reputation as one of Hollywood's most eligible bachelors. They glamorized his height and leanness by frequently referring to him as "a long, cool sip of water." But his height would also help him land his first part in a feature film when MGM's Bill Grady, a casting director with a sense of humor, gave him a role in *Murder Man* (1935) as a reporter named Shortie in ironic counterpoint to his lanky six-foot-three-inch (191cm) frame.

elow: Not only fans but actresses as well liked Jimmy both on and off the set. He was amiable, gentlemanly, easy to work with, and able to establish his own dramatic persona firmly and comfortably on film without upstaging anyone else.

A bove: Jimmy with Jeanette MacDonald and Nelson Eddy in *Rose Marie* (1936). Jimmy played the role of villain only four times in his entire career; the first was as Jeanette MacDonald's no-good younger brother. Although his role was small, it was sufficient to impress a *London Observer* film critic who described Jimmy as "rather like our own Raymond Massey." No one else seemed to observe this particular similarity, although Jimmy was occasionally referred to as a younger version of Gary Cooper. For the most part, from very early on in his career, his style was so uniquely his own that he defied comparison.

R ight: Jimmy with Margaret Sullavan in *Next Time We Love* (1936). Jimmy first met Margaret Sullavan when he worked as stage manager for a production of *The Artist and the Lady*. She had been recruited by Josh Logan. Sullavan would become not only a close friend of Jimmy's but also a costar in four films. She came to Hollywood before Jimmy, signed a contract with Universal, achieved "star" status, and asked for him specifically for a part in *Next Time We Love*. MGM was happy to arrange the loan. Though Jimmy was not billed as the star, he played his first leading role.

Above: Jimmy with Jean Harlow in *Wife Versus Secretary* (1936). As fan mail began to arrive, MGM cast Stewart in a supporting role and gave the male lead to Clark Gable. Jimmy didn't seem to mind, especially since he had to rehearse the kissing scene with Harlow many times over. Kissing Harlow was an experience that would remain in his memory and become a staple in his anecdotes for years to come. *Wife Versus Secretary* marked Jimmy's introduction to Clarence Brown of MGM, who had become famous for his direction of Greta Garbo. Jimmy said it was Brown who made him aware of how important every look and every gesture could be, and how to make the spoken word a "visual" rather than just a verbal experience.

Above: Jimmy in *Born to Dance* (1936). Both Jimmy's comic experience and his crooning at Princeton served him in good stead when he was cast opposite Eleanor Powell. He sang Cole Porter's "Easy to Love" to her in a tenor voice, danced, and demonstrated a growing flair for comedy. Both the song and the film were hits.

Right: Jimmy is shown here with Virginia Bruce who had also appeared with him in *The Murder Man*. Though he was new to musicals, Jimmy's singing and dancing seemed natural, if not distinguished, in his debut in *Born to Dance*. Even Cole Porter, who wrote "Easy to Love" and auditioned Jimmy, thought so. Jimmy was able to hold his own against established stars like Buddy Ebsen (a former vaudevillian) and Eleanor Powell. For an actor who was never thought of as an accomplished vocalist or musician, he would sing and play musical instruments in a surprising number of films, as well as on television.

Opposite: Jimmy with Joan Crawford in *The Gorgeous Hussy* (1936). Jimmy made eight movies in 1936, and was finally cast and billed as the lead in the B film *Speed*, a little-known semi-documentary about the auto industry. For *The Gorgeous Hussy*, he added a southern drawl and sideburns to his repertoire.

Above: Jimmy with Robert Young in *Navy Blue and Gold* (1937). At age twenty-nine, Jimmy still looked a good deal younger than his years, and played the part of a young plebe.

Right: *Navy Blue and Gold*, one of many popular "college films" of the era, tells the story of three young football players, all of whom play a pivotal role in the Army/Navy game. Jimmy is cast true to life, as a dutiful son. Ironically, the Naval Academy in Annapolis had been Jimmy's own first choice for college, although he finally deferred to his father's wishes and he attended Princeton.

Below: Jimmy with Beulah Bondi and Walter Huston in *Of Human Hearts* (1938). Like *Navy Blue and Gold*, *Of Human Hearts* was a dramatic film that would help Stewart define his image onscreen and blur the public's perception of the boundary between the individual and the star. It featured the same small-town roots, the same unconditionally loving mother, the same strong father figure, and a Jimmy who could be tough and angry yet idealistic and innocent. Bondi played his mother with the kind of chemistry that bore repetition in an amazing seven other films, most memorably in *Vivacious Lady* (1938), *Mr. Smith Goes to Washington* (1939), and *It's a Wonderful Life* (1946).

Above: Jimmy Stewart with Margaret Sullavan in *The Shopworn Angel* (1938). This was the second remake of this film; the original was a 1919 silent version, and the first remake was a 1929 partial talkie starring Gary Cooper, Nancy Carroll, and Paul Lucas. One of Jimmy's costars in the film, Walter Pidgeon, observed that Jimmy played the love scenes so convincingly because he was in love with Sullavan in real life. She would eventually marry his friend Henry Fonda.

Top: Jimmy and Hank first met during their time with the University Players in 1932. When the University Players were asked to stage *Carry Nation* in New York, the two roomed together and began an enduring friendship that did not end until Fonda's death in 1992.

Bottom: Jimmy with Jean Arthur in *You Can't Take It with You* (1938). Jimmy took on the role of a lion tamer in this Frank Capra–directed film, which won the Oscar for Best Picture. Jimmy's stature as a star increased not only by association with Capra, who was then at the height of his career, but also because of his skills in madcap comedy. In 1938, Jimmy's career and popularity really began to skyrocket. He also appeared in *Vivacious Lady*, another romantic comedy, with Ginger Rogers.

Above: Jimmy with actor Cary Grant and Frank Capra in 1939. Capra saw both Stewart and Grant as well-suited to portray his comic leads as well as his version of the American everyman, a tough but vulnerable idealist he liked to feature in his dramatic films.

Above: At the prospect of losing his child in this melodramatic scene in *Made For Each Other* (1939), Jimmy was supposed to cry, but the tears would not come, and he ruined several takes in a row. He told gossip columnist Hedda Hopper years later that he didn't have the nerve to ask for "the stuff that makes you cry," so he went outside and held a lit cigarette to his face. After that his eyes were so bloodshot that the scene had to be rescheduled for the next day, when the damage he'd done to his eyes had diminished to a more realistic tearful look.

Right: Jimmy with Joan Crawford and Lew Ayres in *Ice Follies of 1939*. Though Jimmy had originally been considered for the lead in this film, one look at his long, thin legs in tights caused the casting director to put him in a supporting role, where he could wear more flattering baggy pants instead.

Left: Jimmy with Carole Lombard in *Made for Each Other*. When *Made for Each Other* was released, Lombard was one of the most respected actresses in Hollywood. This film required both comedic and dramatic acting, and Carole and Jimmy provided both. In *Made for Each Other*, Jimmy and Carole portray a young married couple struggling with relationship and financial difficulties. When their baby contracts pneumonia they come together to fight the illness, and through a series of extraordinary circumstances they save their child and salvage their relationship.

Left: Jimmy with Claudette Colbert in *It's a Wonderful World* (1939). Many fans don't realize that Jimmy made this little-known screwball comedy, but it was well received and helped to establish his abilities in the type of comedic roles that would soon win him an Academy Award for *The Philadelphia Story* (1940).

Above: Jimmy and Jean Arthur in *Mr. Smith Goes to Washington* (1939). Frank Capra initially wanted Gary Cooper for the role of Jefferson Smith, the young senator and boy scout leader, but Cooper was unavailable. Jimmy proved an excellent second choice. Though controversial at the time because of its negative portrayal of the U.S. Senate, this film would finally elevate Jimmy to superstar status and win him his first Oscar nomination.

Left: Though he was cast in a serious dramatic role in *Mr. Smith Goes to Washington*, Jimmy still had the opportunity to work in some memorable moments of comedy.

Above: Though a parody, *Destry Rides Again* (1939) was Jimmy's first western. His chemistry with Marlene Dietrich, who played the dance hall girl, Frenchy, was unmistakable. She called him *ein fegamer mensch*, a sweet human being. Offscreen, she was one of many female stars who reportedly fell head over heels in love with him.

Opposite, bottom: No matter how hard he tried, Jimmy could not effect the right degree of hoarseness required to make his voice realistic as the filibuster scene wore on in *Mr. Smith Goes to Washington*. So he went to a doctor who placed a few drops of bichloride of mercury on Jimmy's vocal cords. The effect was perfect—Jimmy could hardly even swallow!

A bove: Although the director initially cast an extra for the saloon fight scene in *Destry Rides Again*, Marlene insisted on doing it herself. Jimmy had his hands full trying to dodge her blows.

O pposite: Jimmy dazzled the critics and his fans with his performance as Mike Connor in *The Philadelphia Story* (1940). Following so closely on the heels of *Mr. Smith Goes to Washington*, his acting was considered all the more remarkable. He was terrified of the difficult soliloquy in which he confesses his love to Katharine Hepburn, but famous playwright Noel Coward coached him. The speech was eloquent, inspired, and right in keeping with the peculiarities of his character.

Left: Jimmy and Cary Grant in *The Philadelphia Story*. Jimmy was comfortable enough onscreen now in comic scenes to be able to relax even with the likes of Grant. Together, they improvised the hiccups in the famous champagne scene.

Below: Jimmy and Rosalind Russell in *No Time for Comedy* (1940). Jimmy and Roz just didn't have the kind of chemistry that might have made this film sizzle. It was based on the Broadway hit that starred Laurence Olivier and Katherine Cornell, and suffered in comparison. World War II would soon interrupt Jimmy's busy film career when it was at its zenith—or so it seemed at the time.

Above: Jimmy and Donna Reed, who played the role of Mary Hatch Bailey, his wife, in *It's a Wonderful Life* (1946). They are shown here in the famous scene in which the couple sings "Buffalo Gal" on the way home from the high school prom. The film was Jimmy's personal favorite, and Reed's almost luminous beauty was probably a major factor.

elow: *It's a Wonderful Life* was Jimmy's first film after the war. Jimmy feared he had lost his ability to act, but this film, made under the direction of friend and fellow World War II veteran Frank Capra, proved otherwise. In this scene, the angel Clarence, played by Henry Travers, has just rescued George Bailey from a suicide attempt.

Above: In addition to their passion for acting, Stewart and Fonda shared a hobby: they enjoyed constructing model airplanes and complex kites together. Their similar personalities—very reserved, with a wry wit—were yet another component of their lasting friendship.

Above: In 1939, when Jimmy was nominated for Best Actor by the Academy of Motion Picture Arts and Sciences, he cast his own vote for Hank's performance in *The Grapes of Wrath*. That their friendship endured after this indicated both their deep affection for each other and their professionalism. Many years later, Fonda would win an Oscar for his swan song performance in *On Golden Pond*.

Right: The cub reporter, Shortie, who Jimmy had portrayed so many years ago in *The Murder Man* had truly come of age in his role as Jim McNeal in *Call Northside 777* (1948). McNeil is a character based on real life investigative reporter and Pulitzer Prize winner Jim Maguire who had written a series of articles for the *Chicago Tribune* that eventually cleared an innocent man of murder charges.

Above: Director Alfred Hitchcock saw in Jimmy a potential for sophistication and psychological depth that other directors hadn't really drawn upon fully. He responded more to Jimmy's intelligence and breeding than to his "nice guy" image and cast him accordingly as a college professor in *Rope* (1948). As professor Rupert Cadell, Jimmy solves the case of a grisly murder committed by two of his students, played by Farley Grainger and John Dall.

Left: Jimmy is shown here with Shelley Winters in *Winchester '73* (1950), which marked a turning point in Jimmy's career. It was his first *serious* western. Jimmy is tough, vengeful, obsessive, and cynical as Lin McAdam in this gritty, realistic Anthony Mann film.

Below: Jimmy, who had worked as an independent rather than a contract player since his return from the war, took no salary for his role in *Winchester '73*, mainly because Universal Studios could not afford his asking price of $200,000. Instead, he received 50% of the profit on the film, a landmark arrangement that made him a stakeholder in the film's success and a wealthy man.

Left: Though Jimmy was always known for his political conservatism, he was never afraid of taking on a controversial film, as he had proven before the war with *Mr. Smith Goes to Washington* and *The Mortal Storm* (1940). His role as Tom Jeffords in *Broken Arrow* (1950) demonstrated a personal stand against the injustice perpetrated in America, and particularly in Hollywood, against the Native Americans.

Right: In *Broken Arrow*, Jimmy married the Apache maiden Sonseeahray, played beautifully by Debra Paget. The film also featured Jay Silverheels as Thundercloud, with Jeff Chandler in the role of Cochise.

Above: In *Harvey* (1950), Jimmy played the role of Elwood P. Dowd, an alcoholic who believes that he is always accompanied by a giant white rabbit. There was something in the sheer whimsy and poignancy of that role that resonated with Jimmy's complex personality. He is shown here with a portrait of his pooka friend. Jimmy's relationship with Harvey would become an enduring one, and would always blur the line between fact and fantasy. Years after the film was released, Jimmy was still sketching Harvey between takes on other films, using illustration and cartooning skills that had first surfaced when he was a schoolboy and art editor for the yearbook at Mercersburg. His goal? "To get him just right." He would also work successfully with Harvey again several times on stage and television, in America and in England.

Right: Jimmy was able to make the audience and the senior psychiatrist, Dr. Chumley (played by Cecil Kellaway), believe absolutely in the presence of the mischievous pooka, Harvey.

Below: Jimmy was also able to give his eyes the limpid, semiglazed look of a man who frequently has one too many martinis.

Left: Though Jimmy was at the zenith of his career when the *The Greatest Show on Earth* (1952) was cast, he wanted the part of the clown so badly that he actually offered to work for scale wages. He had loved the circus since he was a boy and he wanted to work with Cecil B. DeMille. To learn the nuances of the role, he studied with the most famous clown of all time, Emmett Kelly, and with several other Ringling greats, and in true circus clown tradition, he designed his own "clown face."

Above: In *The Glenn Miller Story* (1954), Jimmy once again worked with director Anthony Mann, who managed to elicit from the star an almost uncanny resemblance to the bandleader. Unfortunately, this resemblance did not extend to the way Jimmy played the trombone; all of his "playing" had to be dubbed.

Opposite top: Jimmy and June Allison in *The Glenn Miller Story*. The 1950s marked the peak of Jimmy's career, and both he and Allison were top box-office draws, especially as a husband-and-wife team. They also appeared as husband and wife in *The Stratton Story* (1949) and *Strategic Air Command* (1955).

Below: The music may have been dubbed in *The Glenn Miller Story*, but Jimmy's hand movements and mannerisms were seemingly that of a professional musician. Even alongside Louis Armstrong in this scene, Jimmy is thoroughly convincing as bandleader and trombonist Miller.

Above: In *Rear Window* (1954) Jimmy plays the role of voyeuristic L.B. "Jeff" Jeffries, a professional photographer who has broken his leg while he was photographing a race car. Grace Kelly plays Lisa Carol Fremont, his socialite girlfriend. Confined to a wheelchair, Jimmy had to rely almost exclusively on his eyes and range of expression to develop this part.

Opposite: Jimmy and Grace Kelly on the set of *Rear Window*. Jimmy found Grace charming and made plans to appear with her again in *Designing Woman*, but she abandoned her career to marry Prince Ranier of Monaco. Disappointed, Jimmy pulled out of the film and Gregory Peck got the male lead. He was reunited on screen with Grace Kelly years later—not in a film but in video footage—when she sat at his table and participated in the award ceremony in one of her rare American public appearances when he received the AFI's coveted Lifetime Achievement Award.

Above: Jimmy and director Alfred Hitchcock on Ambrose Street in London between takes during the filming of *The Man Who Knew Too Much* (1956), a remake of a 1934 film starring Leslie Banks.

eft: In Alfred Hitchcock's *The Man Who Knew Too Much*, Jimmy plays the morally ambiguous role of a surgeon, Dr. Ben McKenna, with great subtlety. Filmed on location in Marrakech and London, the thriller begins when a dying Frenchman whispers the only clue to an assassination attempt into Jimmy's ear: "Ambrose Chapel."

ight: In *The Spirit of St. Louis* (1957), Jimmy portrayed his own real-life hero, Charles Lindbergh. Producer and friend Leland Howard had wanted a younger actor for the part—Jimmy was almost fifty at the time—but Jimmy and even his father, Alec, pushed hard for the part. Jimmy dieted for the first and maybe the only time in his life, and he had to endure the painful experience of having not only his hair and eyebrows but also his eyelashes bleached to resemble the fair-haired hero who had made the famous flight in his early twenties.

eft: Jimmy's portrayal of Scottie Ferguson in *Vertigo* (1958) is sinister and at times even murderous, as Kim Novak (Madeleine) could attest in this scene in the bell tower at San Juan Batista in San Francisco. Though it was coolly received when it was released, many critics consider *Vertigo* to be Hitchcock's masterpiece and Jimmy's most demanding role and finest performance. It was also the last film they would make together.

Right: Jimmy in 1965 with Lee Remick, his costar in *Anatomy of a Murder* (1959), for which he received his last Academy Award nomination, for his role as country lawyer Paul Biegler. Filmed in black and white for impact and produced and directed by Otto Preminger, it was banned in Chicago by Mayor Daly and in Indiana, Pennsylvania, by Jimmy's father because it was loaded with explicit courtroom language about rape and introduced a pair of women's panties as evidence.

Below: In *Vertigo*, Jimmy's character was obsessed with his love for Judy/Madeleine, both played by Kim Novak. Her sensual, low-keyed acting style suited the mysterious, enigmatic role very well and seemed the perfect foil for Jimmy's intensity. She got the part when Vera Miles became pregnant.

Above: Jimmy with Andy Devine, director John Ford, and John Wayne in *The Man Who Shot Liberty Valance* (1962). Again Jimmy plays a lawyer, but this time one who rises to high office because of a lawless killing erroneously credited to him.

Right: Maureen O'Hara as Mrs. Hobbs with Jimmy in *Mr. Hobbs Takes a Vacation* (1962). Jimmy plays a first-time grandfather in this comedy about family life.

Below: Jimmy appears here as the rugged but reliable trapper Linus Rawlings with Debbie Reynolds and Brigid Bazlin in *How the West Was Won* (1963), a star-studded family odyssey narrated by Spencer Tracy that spanned an epic period between 1839 and 1889.

Above: Sandra Dee played daughter Molly Michaelson to Jimmy's dotty Frank Michaelson in *Take Her, She's Mine* (1963), a film that featured a running gag in which people confuse Frank for Jimmy Stewart and are always asking him for autographs. Though Jimmy looks stern in this photograph, the film was a typical 1960s comedy.

Above: By the time Jimmy made *Shenandoah* (1965) he had achieved the stature of patriarch both on and off the screen. He is shown here in character for the part of Charlie Anderson.

Left: This still features a shot of Jimmy with his beloved horse, Pi, in *Shenandoah*. The two made many westerns together. Henry Fonda painted a portrait of Pi, which became one of Jimmy's most prized possessions.

Above: Jimmy as Frank Towns, the pilot who flies oil men who work in the Sahara Desert back to civilization in *The Flight of the Phoenix* (1966). This was Jimmy's fifth aviation-related film and featured a distinguished ensemble cast, including Hardy Kruger, Richard Attenborough, Peter Finch, Ernest Borgnine, Dan Duryea, and George Kennedy, among others.

Left: John Wayne's role as terminally ill cowboy John Bernard Books in *The Shootist* (1976) mirrored his condition in real life. Jimmy, who had been turning roles down at that time, quickly accepted the part of Doc Hostetler when he heard of Wayne's decision to go ahead with the film. The relationship of these two legends and their mutual recognition of Wayne's condition gave a special poignancy to the film, which has been called "an elegy for a cowboy."

Below: Jimmy and Henry Fonda in *The Cheyenne Social Club* (1970), one of the first of the "buddy" films that would become so popular in the 1970s. The film also starred Shirley Jones.

Chapter Three

The Pilot and the Hero

Opposite: Jimmy's interest in airplanes began when he was a very young boy and continued throughout his life. In his senior year at Princeton, he was awarded the D'Amato Prize, a scholarship for graduate school tuition presented to the student who demonstrated "the greatest promise in architectural design." The basis for this award was his senior thesis, an airport design complete with hangar, which demonstrated both his passion for aviation and his skill at architectural drawing.

Above: Jimmy had gotten his pilot's license as soon as he had a regular paycheck in Hollywood. He flew home to Indiana, Pennsylvania, frequently in his early days as a star, navigating by the railroad tracks. When American involvement in World War II seemed inevitable, he began logging more and more hours in the air so that he would be eligible for pilot's training in the military.

Above: Jimmy being sworn into the Army Air Force. Nothing in Stewart's life had a more profound influence on him than his involvement in World War II. He was thirty-three years old earning $3,000 a week as one of Hollywood's most rapidly rising stars; he needn't have been involved in the war at all. When he was drafted initially, he failed to meet the weight requirement for a man of his height, and was given a deferment. He appealed his deferral and finally met the weight requirement—by one ounce (28g), according to some stories. Other versions say he still couldn't quite meet the requirement but managed to talk his way in anyway, while many other leading men in Hollywood were trying to talk their way out.

Above: Just before Jimmy shipped out in October 1943, his parents visited him in Sioux City. Jimmy's father gave him a copy of the Ninety-first Psalm to carry with him. In a note that accompanied the psalm, he told Jimmy how much he loved him. Jimmy cherished both throughout the war and often read the psalm and letter for comfort.

Left: Another MGM superstar, Clark Gable, had enlisted after his wife, Carole Lombard, was killed in a plane crash on a trip to sell war bonds. Captain Gable also saw active duty overseas and participated in bombing raids.

Left: On April 8, 1944, Jimmy was awarded the Air Medal. He also received the United States Army Air Force's Distinguished Flying Cross on May 3, 1944, for his leadership during the raids on Brunswick, Germany, in February, as well as the *croix de guerre* from the French government.

Below: One of the reasons the Army Air Force wanted to keep Jimmy out of harm's way was his tremendous popularity. His films were well known and loved throughout the United States and Europe. The British and French particularly loved *Mr. Smith Goes to Washington*, one of a number of Jimmy's films banned by Hitler during the war.

Opposite: Jimmy was promoted to the rank of brigadier general in 1959. He would remain active with the reserves for many years after the war; when he retired in 1968, he was presented with the Distinguished Service Medal. But the war had taken its toll on Jimmy. He had been a hero, but it was his fear he spoke of, if he spoke at all, and not his feats of bravery. He would not allow the press or studios to capitalize on his war record and refused to be cast in military roles. He eventually took a part as an officer in a war zone in *The Mountain Road* (1960), but this was the only "war" film in which he would ever appear.

Chapter Four

Husband and Father

Opposite: For many years, Jimmy had dated the most glamorous women in Hollywood, but none of his romances ever led to marriage. Then, after the war, he met Gloria Hatrick McLean. She was beautiful, poised, urbane, and witty. She also shared Jimmy's love of the great outdoors, golf, and animals. Perhaps most importantly to Jimmy, she was not an actress. Gloria was born in Larchmont, New York, in 1919. Her father, a Hearst executive, had helped pioneer movie house newsreels. Here they are shown with Bello, Gloria's pet at the time of their courtship.

Above: At the time of his marriage Jimmy was forty-one years old and was considered such an elusive bachelor that Walter Winchell once quipped that the star's courtship of Gloria generated more news coverage than Orson Welles' famous radio broadcast of *The War Between the Worlds*. They were married at the Brentwood Presbyterian Church on August 9, 1948.

Above: Bill Grady, one of Jimmy's close friends, was Jimmy's best man. Gloria's sister, Ruth Draddy, served as her attendant.

Above: On their first date Jimmy took Gloria golfing. She won, but he didn't seem to mind because he kept asking her out for more golf dates. She finally had to remind him that she did eat as well as play golf, after which he began taking her out to dinner, too.

Left: Jimmy and Gloria loved to vacation in exotic locations, such as Mexico, Hawaii, and Africa. He was pleasantly surprised to be recognized as far away as the Chinese border in the Far East. During the 1960s, Jimmy and Gloria spent a lot of time in Africa and eventually became very active in efforts to preserve endangered wildlife.

Left: Gloria, who was divorced, brought two sons to the marriage, so Jimmy had a ready-made family when he married her. Ronald McLean (right) was born in 1943, Michael McLean (left) in 1946.

Below: Michael, Ron, Gloria, Jimmy, and their dog, Bello, are shown on the front lawn of the family home on Roxbury Drive in Beverly Hills. Jimmy liked to cut the grass himself and Gloria was an avid gardener.

Opposite: Jimmy not only made films, he also traveled extensively to promote them. Gloria was his constant companion, and she sometimes even went on location with him, as she did when he was filming *The Man Who Knew Too Much* (1956) in Marrakech and London.

ight: Twin daughters Judy and Kelly were born on May 7, 1951, at Cedars of Lebanon Hospital. Jimmy was delighted. He was also so excited (or absentminded) that he forgot to go back to pick Gloria up from her hospital room after he took her bags to the car. Instead he drove to a store to check out a new camera to take better shots of his newly enlarged family. Only when the salesman told him that the camera was simple enough for his wife to use did Jimmy remember that Gloria was still waiting for him at the hospital.

Left: The Stewart family loved the large library/TV room in the house on Roxbury Drive; it was their favorite gathering place. The house also had five bedrooms. Gloria had thought it looked like a dormitory when they first looked at the house during her pregnancy. Jimmy's response was, "That's what we need, isn't it?"

Above: (Left to right) Jimmy, Judy, Gloria, Kelly, and Michael with his date. In this informal family shot from the late 1960s, son Ronald is sadly absent. A marine lieutenant, he was killed in Vietnam on June 11, 1967.

Right: Gloria enjoyed photo opportunities and guest appearances every bit as much as Jimmy did. After attending Finch College in New York City, she had entered some beauty contests and studied acting, for a while considering a career onstage. Instead she had wed and then divorced Ned McLean II, whose mother had owned the Hope diamond.

Above: The Stewarts were one of Hollywood's happiest and most photogenic couples. Gloria, always elegantly attired, never told Jimmy what she spent on her wardrobe. He preferred comfortable rather than stylish clothing and spent a good deal of time returning clothes she had given him as gifts. He never saw the need for something new when what he already had was still perfectly wearable.

Right: As Jimmy's film persona became darker and more complex after the war, frequent guest appearances with Gloria on television in venues such as *The Jack Benny Show* and *The Dean Martin Show* reassured his audience that his personal and family values had not changed. An anomaly in Hollywood, he was very happily married, went to church, had a growing family, and, no matter what roles he took, forever remained the same reliable Jimmy Stewart.

Left: Jimmy and Gloria's love affair continued for more than forty-five years until her death in 1994, after which he retired completely from public life.

Chapter Five

Television

Opposite: Jimmy launched his own television series in 1971: a weekly situation comedy called *The Jimmy Stewart Show*. He had wanted Gloria to play the part of his wife, but NBC nixed the idea. Forty-four-year-old Julie Adams was cast in the part. Jimmy was in his sixties at the time.

Above: Jimmy played James Howard, an accordion-playing, absentminded anthropology professor with a dog and a multigenerational family that included Jonathan Daly as his eldest son, Ellen Geer as his daughter-in-law, Dennis Larson as his eight-year-old son, and Kirby Furlong as his grandson. The show aired for only one season.

eft and below: Jimmy first appeared on *The Tonight Show Starring Johnny Carson* on the show's seventeenth anniversary, in 1979. These in-depth, very personal conversations brought him to the awareness of a newer, younger audience and enabled him to remain highly visible. He became more than a movie star because of these appearances. People began to see him as a cherished friend with a family and pets and feelings and ideas he sometimes expressed in poetry. Carson loved Jimmy's wry, charming wit and his self-caricatures.

Above: Television also served to make Stewart an icon in other ways. When stations began to air *It's a Wonderful Life* frequently during the holiday season, the film became as much of a classic as *A Christmas Carol*. Jimmy's voice-over ads for Campbell's Soup were also extraordinarily successful. The emergence of cable television stations such as American Movie Classics and Turner Classic Movies also kept him in the public eye.

Chapter Six

Awards and Honors

Opposite: Jimmy Stewart and Ginger Rogers appeared together at the 1940 Oscars, where she won Best Actress for her performance in *Kitty Foyle* and he took Best Actor for *The Philadelphia Story*.

Above: One of Jimmy's favorite stories was about how his father took possession of the Oscar for display in the hardware store back in Indiana, Pennsylvania. In the wee hours of the morning after Jimmy won the coveted award, Alec called on the phone and asked Jimmy to describe it; he then directed Jimmy to send it home. Ever the dutiful son, Jimmy did, where it remained on display until his father's death in 1968.

Right: Jimmy and Capra became very close friends for life. Here, they pose for photographers at a luncheon in 1985, which was held to honor the Oscar-winning director for his lifetime achievement in the motion picture industry.

Below: On March 25, 1985, Jimmy was the proud recipient of an honorary Lifetime Achievement Oscar. It was presented to him by former costar and film great Cary Grant, who spoke of Jimmy's "decency, strength, and kindness."

Above: Friend and former actor Ronald Reagan bestowed the Presidential Medal of Freedom on Jimmy in May 1985. It is considered America's highest civilian honor.

Left: Jimmy is seen here testifying in front of a congressional committee on June 15, 1988, on several issues very dear to his heart related to the preservation of classic films. He particularly decried the colorization of films, which he considered a desecration of the art of light and shadow so carefully and painstakingly wrought in black-and-white films.

Conclusion

There may never have been a star who was as real to his audience as Jimmy was, and to such a large and diverse audience at that. He was admired, yes, but he was also loved. Perhaps because his audience had shared so many meaningful moments with him in his films, moments they defined as "theirs," people felt and acted like they knew him personally.

Generally regarded as *the* quintessential nice guy of American cinema, Jimmy was labeled "a natural" at his chosen profession by critics, fans, and even friends. This comment, intended as a compliment, always annoyed him and there are many, many interviews throughout the years in which he tried patiently to explain that he had always had to work hard at his chosen profession. He said, "People call me a natural-born actor, and I get mad. I say there's nothing natural about a camera, lights, and forty or fifty people standing around watching you all the time. It's hard. And if I give a natural performance on the screen, you can be damn well sure I'm working at it."

In reality, he was such a great actor that people just didn't realize he was acting. He even fooled the film critics. Such a master of illusion was he, so skilled at bringing people right into the emotion and reality he was somehow creating for them onscreen in that moment, that people thought they were just watching Jimmy Stewart play Jimmy Stewart again.

The question then is: *which* Jimmy Stewart? The "George Bailey" Jimmy Stewart in *It's a Wonderful Life* or the "Elwood P. Dowd" Jimmy Stewart in *Harvey*? These were certainly both defining roles for him, yet they were very different. Directors Frank Capra, Alfred Hitchcock, Anthony Mann, and John Ford, to name a few, all saw very different Jimmy Stewarts, and so did we, the audience, if we watched more than a handful of the eighty-plus films he made in a career that spanned six decades.

The ironic result of his film career was that he was almost universally well received as a person and entertainer, but that Jimmy Stewart was not generally perceived to be a great actor. Despite a handful of Academy Award nominations, two Oscars, and enough other prestigious acting awards to fill a gallery in his museum, it bears repeating—he is rarely thought of as a great actor.

Instead, he is better known and loved among his legion of fans for his decency than his acting abilities. Somehow the acting seemed incidental to the goodness people perceived in him, and the many movies in which he played dark and even sinister roles—and played them superbly—just don't figure into the public's memory or perception of him.

Some said he had a rather "narrow range." Unlike many of his costars, he never tried his hand at producing or directing, except for one television show. The talent wasn't lacking, but the interest was. Jimmy simply preferred the other side of the camera.

Certainly, he knew his own range well enough not to attempt Shakespeare, epics, swashbucklers, or horror movies, but he played almost every other genre and a lot of different kinds of roles in each. When you watch even a random handful of his films, you see that he played a number of these very diverse roles brilliantly.

He was one of an elite few ever to win an Academy Award for Best Actor in a comic role. Though he never thought he was "all that good" in his Oscar-winning role as Mike Connor in *The Philadelphia Story* (1940), it would be hard to imagine any other actor pulling off the difficult "there's a magnificence in you, Tracy" speech to Katharine Hepburn. Nor should it be forgotten that he and Cary Grant improvised the entire hiccup scene, and had a good time doing it. Following his nomination the year before for his breakthrough dramatic role as Jefferson Smith in *Mr. Smith Goes to Washington*, who would have guessed he had an equally intense flair for madcap comedy within that "narrow range"?

Though many actors have been very closely identified with a particular role or type, never was there one who played so many different types and yet remained so closely identified with so few as Jimmy Stewart. His directors and producers reinforced this to some extent: he was cast as a bad guy in only four of the more than eighty films he made, but he played morally ambiguous characters in more than twenty films.

What did he think about this? We'll never really know. He was, as the saying goes, a very private person. He never wrote an autobiography or authorized a critical biography, and he never read one that was written about him, though there are many. Typically, it is the writers who resist biographies most strenuously and not the stars, especially not a star who had perhaps one of the cleanest consciences and brightest records in all of Hollywood.

We do know from statements he made in interviews that he thought an abundance of praise, even if it is deserved, could swell a person's head, and he wanted none of that. He didn't believe in intellectualizing about his performances, whether they were good, bad, or indifferent (he was an experiential and not an intellectual actor anyway).

Perhaps he simply knew what we all know about him: you can never really capture the magic in words, in a timeline of events, in a characterization of a life, in the facts and figures and fables. It had been a wonderful life, he said. From it, a legend and an institution had emerged and spun a veil, to quote writer James Hillman. And the magician in Jimmy Stewart liked that veil and kept it pretty well intact by eschewing biography and remaining true to his own character and calling.

He began his career as a matinee idol, became a legend, and ended his long life as an American institution. So much has been written about him, about his talent and work and decency and patriotism and family values and sense of humor. But he was more than the sum of all of that, and we were all the richer for what he was. When Jimmy Stewart died on July 2, 1997, President Bill Clinton spoke for fans the world over when he said, "We have lost a national treasure."

Above: Active well into his eighties, Jimmy died on July 2, 1997, one of the very last of an extraordinary generation of legends of the silver screen. He once said that if he had to write his own epitaph it would be, "He sure gave us a lot of pleasure over the course of the years." He surely did.

Television Productions

The Windmill, General Electric Theater. CBS, April 24, 1955.

The Town with a Past, General Electric Theater. CBS, February 10, 1957.

The Trail to Christmas, General Electric Theater. CBS, December 15, 1957.

Cindy's Fella, Ford Startime Theater. NBC, December 15, 1959.

Flashing Spikes, Alcoa premiere. ABC, October 4, 1962.

The Jimmy Stewart Show (series). NBC, 1971–1972.

Harvey, Hallmark Hall of Fame. NBC, March 21, 1972.

Hawkins on Murder (pilot). CBS, March 13, 1973.

Hawkins (miniseries). CBS, 1973–1974.
   Mr. Krueger's Christmas. Syndicated, December 21, 1980.

Right of Way. HBO, November 21, 1983.

North and South Book II. ABC, May 6, 1986.

In addition to these productions, Jimmy Stewart made numerous guest appearances on television shows, including *The Jack Benny Show*, *The Tonight Show Starring Johnny Carson*, and the final episode of *The Carol Burnett Show*.

Stage Credits

Carry Nation. Biltmore Theater, 1932.

Goodbye Again. Theater Masque, 1932.

Spring in Autumn. Henry Miller Theater, 1933.

All Good Americans. Henry Miller Theater, 1933.

Yellow Jack. Martin Beck Theater, 1934.

Divided by Three. Ethel Barrymore Theater, 1934.

Page Miss Glory. Mansfield Theater, 1934.

Journey by Night. Shubert Theater, 1935.

Harvey. 48th Street Theater, 1947.

Harvey. ANTA Theater, 1970.

Harvey. Prince of Wales Theater (London), 1975.

Filmography

Art Trouble. Vitaphone, 1934.

Important News. MGM Miniature, 1935.

Murder Man. MGM, 1935.

Rose Marie. MGM, 1936.

Next Time We Love. Universal, 1936.

Wife Versus Secretary. MGM, 1936.

Small Town Girl. MGM, 1936.

Speed. MGM, 1936.

The Gorgeous Hussy. MGM, 1936.

Born to Dance. MGM, 1936.

After the Thin Man. MGM, 1936.

Seventh Heaven. Twentieth Century-Fox, 1937.

The Last Gangster. MGM, 1937.

Navy Blue and Gold. MGM, 1937.

Of Human Hearts. MGM, 1938.

Vivacious Lady. RKO, 1938.

The Shopworn Angel. MGM, 1938.

You Can't Take It with You. Columbia, 1938.

Made for Each Other. United Artists, 1939.

Ice Follies of 1939. MGM, 1939.

It's a Wonderful World. MGM, 1939.

Mr. Smith Goes to Washington. Columbia, 1939.

Destry Rides Again. Universal, 1939.

The Shop Around the Corner. MGM, 1940.

The Mortal Storm. MGM, 1940.

No Time for Comedy. Warner Brothers, 1940.

The Philadelphia Story. MGM, 1940.

Come Live with Me. MGM, 1941.

Pot o' Gold. United Artists, 1941.

Ziegfeld Girl. MGM, 1941.

It's a Wonderful Life. Liberty Films/RKO, 1946.

Magic Town. RKO, 1947.

Call Northside 777. Twentieth Century-Fox, 1948.

On Our Merry Way (A Miracle Can Happen). United Artists, 1948.

Rope. Warner Brothers, 1948.

You Gotta Stay Happy. Universal, 1948.

The Stratton Story. MGM, 1949.

Malaya. MGM, 1949.

Winchester '73. Universal, 1950.

Broken Arrow. Twentieth Century-Fox, 1950.

The Jackpot. Twentieth Century-Fox, 1950.

Harvey. Universal, 1950.

No Highway in the Sky. Twentieth Century-Fox, 1951.

The Greatest Show on Earth. Paramount, 1952.

Bend of the River. Universal, 1952.

Carbine Williams. MGM, 1952.

The Naked Spur. MGM, 1952.

Thunder Bay. Universal, 1953.

The Glenn Miller Story. Universal, 1954.

Rear Window. Paramount, 1954.

The Far Country. Universal, 1954.

Strategic Air Command. Paramount, 1955.

The Man from Laramie. Columbia, 1955.

The Man Who Knew Too Much. Paramount, 1956.

The Spirit of St. Louis. Warner Brothers, 1957.

Night Passage. Universal, 1957.

Vertigo. Paramount, 1958.

Bell, Book and Candle. Columbia, 1959.

Anatomy of a Murder. Columbia, 1959.

The FBI Story. Warner Brothers, 1959.

The Mountain Road. Columbia, 1960.

Two Rode Together. Columbia, 1961.

X-15. United Artists, 1961.

The Man Who Shot Liberty Valance. Paramount, 1962.

Mr. Hobbs Takes a Vacation. Twentieth Century-Fox, 1962.

How the West Was Won. MGM, 1963.

Take Her, She's Mine. Twentieth Century-Fox, 1963.

Cheyenne Autumn. Warner Brothers, 1964.

Dear Brigitte. Twentieth Century-Fox, 1965.

Shenandoah. Universal, 1965.

The Flight of the Phoenix. Twentieth Century-Fox, 1966.

The Rare Breed. Universal, 1966.

Firecreek. Warner Brothers, 1968.

Bandolero! Twentieth Century-Fox, 1968.

The Cheyenne Social Club. National General, 1970.

Fool's Parade. Columbia, 1971.

That's Entertainment. MGM, 1974.

The Shootist. Warner Brothers, 1976.

Airport '77. Universal, 1977.

The Magic of Lassie. International Picture Show Co., 1978.

The Big Sleep. Wincast/ITC, 1978.

A Tale of Africa (The Green Horizon). Sanrio Communications, 1981.

Right of Way. HBO, 1983.

An American Tail: Fievel Goes West. Amblin/Universal, 1990.

Bibliography

BOOKS

Allyson, June, with Francis Spatz Leighton. *June Allyson*. New York: G. P. Putnam's Sons, 1982.

Bach, Steven. *Marlene Dietrich: Life and Legend*. New York: William Morrow & Co., 1992.

Basinger, Jeanine. *The It's a Wonderful Life Book*. New York: Alfred A. Knopf, 1989

Dewey, Donald. *James Stewart: A Biography*. Atlanta: Turner Publishing, Inc., 1996.

Eyles, Allen. *James Stewart*. New York: Stein and Day, 1984.

Fishgall, Gary. *Pieces of Time: The Life of James Stewart*. New York: Scribner, 1997.

Hillman, James. *The Soul's Code in Search of Character and a Calling*. New York: Random House, 1997.

Holden, Anthony. *Behind the Oscars*. New York: Simon & Schuster, 1993.

Katz, Ephraim. *The Film Encyclopedia*. New York: Harper Perennial, 1994.

Molyneaux, Gerard. *James Stewart: A Bio-Bibliography*. Westport, Conn.: Greenwood Press, 1992.

Pickard, Roy. *Jimmy Stewart: A Life in Film*. New York: St. Martin's Press, 1992.

Sarris, Andrew. *The Primal Screen*. New York: Simon and Schuster, 1973.

Speck, Gregory. *Hollywood Royalty*. New York: Birch Lane, 1992.

Spoto, Donald. *The Dark Side of Genius: The Life of Alfred Hitchcock*. Boston: Little, Brown, 1993.

Stewart, James. *Jimmy Stewart and His Poems*. New York: Crown Publishers, 1989.

Wiley, Mason, and Damien Bona. *Inside Oscar: The Unofficial History of the Academy Awards*. New York: Ballantine, 1986.

NEWSPAPERS, MAGAZINES, PRESS RELEASES, AND UNPUBLISHED MATERIAL

Bogdanovich, Peter. "The Respawnsibility of being J...Jimmy Stewart. Gosh!" *Esquire*, July 1966.

Fonda, Henry as told to Howard Teichmann. *Fonda, My Life*. New York: New American Library, Inc., 1981.

Freeman, David. "The Last American." *Buzz*, August 1997.

Harbison, Georgia, and Jeffrey Ressner. "A Wonderful Fella." *Time*, July 14, 1997.

Kennedy, Ward. *Pageant*, January 1992.

Martin, Pete. "The Shyest Guy in Hollywood." *The Saturday Evening Post*, September 15, 1951.

Mc-Coy-Jones Allison and Ellen von Karajan. "A Biography: James Maitland Stewart." News release prepared as part of The Jimmy Stewart Museum's exhibit at the dedication of The Jimmy Stewart Film Theater at Princeton University, May, 1997.

Mullins, Jessie. "So Long, Stalwart Rider." *American Cowboy*, September/October 1997.

Reed, Rex, "The Old Codger Slows Down." *New York Daily News*, October 23, 1977.

Sobran, Joseph. "A Gift Apart From the Usual." *Washington (D.C.) Times*, July 8, 1997.

Swauger, Craig, and Jan Woodard. *Jimmy Stewart: Commemorative Program*. Indiana, PA: The Jimmy Stewart Museum, 1995.

Thomas, Kevin. "Movie Making—30 Years of Fun for Jimmy Stewart." *Los Angeles Times*, October 15, 1977.

Universal Studios. Press release for *The Glenn Miller Story*, 1954.

Von Karajan, Ellen. Audiocassette tour. The Jimmy Stewart Museum, 1997.

Wills, Garry. "Two Sides of Innocence." *Time*, July 14, 1997.

Photography Credits

Archive Photo: pp. 11, 26, 48 bottom, 55 top, 66 top, 71 bottom, 77 both, 80 top

Archive Photo/American Stock: p. 25 top

Corbis-Bettmann: pp. 15, 16 top, 17, 20, 21, 42 bottom, 68

Doc Pele/Stills/Retna Limited U.S.A.: pp. 63, 65 top

Kobal Collection: pp. 12, 19, 23, 24, 27 bottom, 29 top, 30, 31, 32 bottom, 33, 41, 42 top, 45, 53, 56, 58, 59 bottom, 64, 65 bottom, 66 bottom, 72 bottom, 74, 79 bottom, 84, 87

Museum of Modern Art Film Still Archives: pp. 8, 29 bottom, 34 top, 38 both, 39, 40, 43, 46 left, 46–47, 50 top, 51, 52 both, 54, 57, 59 top, 60, 61 bottom, 78, 79 top, 80 bottom

Michael Ochs Archive/Venice, CA: pp. 9, 32 top, 81 both

Penguin/Corbis-Bettmann: pp. 14, 35 top

Photofest: pp. 2, 6, 22 bottom, 25 bottom, 27 top, 34–35 center, 36, 37, 49, 50 bottom, 61 top, 67, 83 top, 85

Popperfoto/Archive: pp. 55 bottom, 62 top

Seely G. Mudd Library/Princeton University: pp. 18, 22 top

Retna Limited U.S.A.: ©Holland: p. 28; ©Urli/Stills: p. 93

Reuters/Corbis-Bettmann: p. 83 bottom

Springer/Corbis-Bettmann: pp. 16 bottom, 44, 48 top

UPI/Corbis-Bettmann: pp. 10, 62 bottom, 69, 70, 71 top, 72 top, 73, 75, 76, 82, 86 both, 88, 89, 90 both, 91 both

Index